DEDICATION

This book is dedicated to YOU!

Welcome and Congratulations for choosing YOU!

YOU, who is courageous enough to take the time to EXPLORE your thoughts.

YOU, who boldly leaves normal behind and takes inspired action to TRANSFORM your life.

YOU, who knows deep down you deserve to FLOURISH!

YOU are the writer of your life and this journal is the process of writing your life.

"New year- a new chapter, new verse or just the same old story? Ultimately we write it. The choice is ours"

–ALEX MORRITT

Love yourself enough to turn the page.......

INTRODUCTION

"What is necessary to change a person is to change his awareness of himself"
–ABRAHAM MASLOW

I was on the same treadmill as everyone else, addicted to the busyness of life; feeling good by doing for others and leaving my own needs and wants at the bottom of my' to do' list, often unfulfilled. I had the sole responsibility of raising three children alone and as a secondary school teacher I commuted half an hour from home. I was involved in a nasty separation with my ex with the stress of parenting responsibilities, court appearances and mounting financial costs and I was burned out, depressed and broke!

We've been taught we can have the life we dream of... that the world is our oyster if we just work hard enough. We've also been taught to put others first as caring human beings. I was on that treadmill, hurried and harried, attempting to do it all; standing up for my children in court, being a good teacher, parent, daughter and friend. From my perspective it looked like others had it all going on, succeeding in life and I felt I couldn't seem to manage, let alone get ahead. I got stuck in the facade of pretending I was fine, not daring to stop for fear of tipping my hand and showing my vulnerability. I just kept keeping on until I couldn't any more.

Even in the busyness, I knew I needed time for myself and I did what I could for my health. This was far from a new concept for me, having been a competitive swimmer in my youth and dedicated to the pursuit of wellness, both in my undergrad degree in kinesiology and the driving force in my lifestyle and career pursuits. The challenge was how to make personal wellbeing a priority while rushing to and fro in my "jobs", both paid and unpaid. I was like so many of us, and only seemed to find the time for 'me' when every thing else was completed on my 'to do' list.

Eventually and reluctantly, I had to take time off from teaching for my emotional and physical health. In pushing pause, free from some of life's stress, I was reminded again that my health had to be a priority for me and for my children, as the responsible present parent. To help them, I had to help myself first!

Fast forward into the future and I, again, started to feel the time pressure to fit everything I felt I 'should' do into my day. Despite the growing awareness of the need to practice self care, supporting what I already believed, I was unhealthy, unhappy and conflicted in finding the time and energy for life's responsibilities and taking care of me. I believe the phrase, 'practicing self care' is part of the problem. It suggests a one off, a need to find some time within our day and week to take care of ourselves, and it essentially becomes another task in our already hectic busy life. I prefer a focus on prioritizing our personal wellbeing that then becomes the basis from which we make all our decisions and lifestyle choices.

I retired early, being proactive about my own health and passionate about helping others and I wrote my first book: Explore, Transform. Flourish : Support and Hope for Those Who Help Others. It was my answer to the self care 'problem'. It encourages us to boldly go where we've not allowed ourselves to go before and put ourselves first and prioritize our well being. It introduces the Flourish process; an eight step formula for being solution focused in making a personal or professional change. The Flourish process, although it requires self reflection and a focus on you, the underlying belief is that putting ourselves first, doesn't exclude others. When we consider our wants and needs first, we are happier and healthier and that leads to encouraging others to do the same. It's the opposite of the paradigm in which we grew up.... thinking of and doing for yourself first is selfish. Do for others first and never mind if that means sacrificing your health and happiness.

Now more than ever these present times have shown us it's up to us to create our health and the life we want. Now is the time to do it differently! It's time for you! For us! That what we want and need to support our health and happiness isn't as a just reward for helping tirelessly or as a last resort when and if we have the time. Let's shift the paradigm so it becomes accepted practice to value ourselves as much as we value those we help.

This book provides inspiration that encourages action! Journals provide opportunities to explore our thoughts, our beliefs and our experiences however there's no transformation without the action. More accurately this book is a guide toward achieving eudaimonia; human flourishing. Flourishing is living our life to the fullest and that requires three things:
1. Becoming the best person you can be
2. Doing the inner work to truly 'know thyself'
3. Taking action and applying your unique gifts and talents in life for the good of yourself and others

The journal is divided into three sections; Explore, Transform, Flouish and then further subdivided into the eight steps of the flourishing process.

- *F*ocus
- *L*ove
- *O*wn It
- *U*nity
- *R*esponsibility
- *I*nspiration
- *S*ynergy
- *H*armony

Each entry is complete with an inspirational quote, a journal prompt and then a suggested inspired action for the day. The second page includes a power mantra, intention setting and gratitude sections and you end your day reflecting on reasons to celebrate, what you learned, what you would change and what you are looking forward to tomorrow.

My wishes for you: May you have the courage and take the time to get to know YOU. Believing you matter and that in transforming your life, you make a difference in the world. May you experience as much joy on this journey as I had in writing this book for you. There is no transformation without action, and the reason I wrote this journal to companion my first book.

Happy exploring.
Here's to flourishing.
Much love,
Gillian

HOW TO GET THE MOST FROM THIS BOOK

1. Feel free to skip around. Although there's a process, it's fine to complete the entries in the order that resonates with you. This is your SELF guided journal. Take what you want and leave the rest.

2. Happiness is an inside job; a choice, a state of being and it doesn't mean you deny your other feelings. Emotions are just energy in motion.

3. Journalling allows for reflection. When you stop thinking and allow by responding to the prompt and just writing you gain access to your inner most thoughts.

4. We change our mood, by changing our body, and vice versa. The Inspired Action section was designed to inspire transformation.

5. Focus on the power mantra for the day. Be conscious of your words. Any words following the words 'I AM' are your truth.

6. Set intentions over goals, written in present tense. They become more of a 'must' than a 'should' and you increase your chance of achieving them with that focus.

7. When you are in a state of gratefulness you attract more to be grateful for. You could add the words 'now that" after 'I'm so happy and grateful to indicate what you desire has already happened.

8. The Day's End section provides perspective about your day and life and with the nightly affirmation, it's a focus for your subconscious as you sleep.

9. There are a variety of worksheets, for added focus, and blank pages for your brainstorming and to keep track of your 'a-ha' moments, learning and resources. Make this yours.

> *These recent times have shown us that we're not returning to the ways things were. We're leaving normal, as a society. My hope is that one person at a time, we'll move from " I" to "Us". This journal is SELF guided, honouring you, and your uniqueness while knowing that as each of us achieves eudaimonia, we transform our lives and our world.*

Leaving Normal; Start Where You Are!

"The opportunity of our times is for each one of us to understand at a very personal level, that we can have a profound impact on the world in which we live. The greatest possibilities for global transformation exist in the fabric of our individual lives."

–LENEDRA J. CARROLL

> "You don't fear change. You fear the unknown. If you knew the future would be great, you'd welcome the change to get there. Well, the future IS great."
>
> –JOE VITALE

I could

_____

_____

_____

_____

Inspired Action

DREAM! You have to start somewhere. What would you change this in year in the areas of health, happiness, relationships, prosperity and success? Jot your ideas down on the 'Life I'm Dreaming Of' page at the end of this section. You can adapt and add to it whenever as change happens. Woot woot!

I AM strong, courageous and worthy of all good.

Today, I intend	*I'm so happy and grateful*
1.	1.
2.	2.
3.	3.

Day's End

I celebrate

I learned

I would change

*T*omorrow, I look forward to

I AM flourishing! I AM love, health, abundance, joy and success!

EXPLORE, TRANSFORM, FLOURISH COMPANION JOURNAL

"Burnout is an erosion of the soul and the soul's need to be living the life you were meant to live, accompanied by the feeling that regardless of what you do you cannot make a difference in the workplace"

–JANE SIMINGTON

I can relate

_____

_____

_____

_____

Inspired Action

PUSH PAUSE! If time and money were unlimited what would you do to feed your soul? Use the notes section at the back of the book to free write. Start with the basics in taking care of the skin you're in and aim to drink eight glasses of water with a pinch of sea salt to hydrate and benefit from the minerals in the salt. Taking care of your body is essential or where will you live?

I have all the time in the world to do what I am here to do.

Today, I intend	*I'm so happy and grateful*
1.	1.
2.	2.
3.	3.

Day's End

I celebrate

I learned

I would change

*T*omorrow, I look forward to

I AM flourishing! I AM love, health, abundance, joy and success!

"Laugh and your cells laugh with you"
–CARI CORBETT- OWEN

*H*ow can I enhance my sense of humour?

_____

_____

_____

_____

Inspired Action

LISTEN TO YOUR BODY! Where do you feel tense, strong, worried, energetic, uncomfortable, healthy? Increase your awareness of how your body feels and act on those valuable insights. Laugh more today and feel your energy surge. Your body will glow if you dry brush to increase circulation and exfoliate at the same time. Our skin is the biggest detox organ.

All my cells are vibrating with energy and I AM healthy and happy.

Today, I intend	I'm so happy and grateful
1.	1.
2.	2.
3.	3.

Day's End

I celebrate

I learned

I would change

*T*omorrow, I look forward to

I AM flourishing! I AM love, health, abundance, joy and success!

"Happiness cannot be travelled to, owned, earned, worn or consumed. Happiness is the spiritual experience of living every minute with love, grace and gratitude."

–DENIS WAITLEY

I'll be happy when

_____

_____

_____

_____

Inspired Action

SMILE! Do you suffer from 'I'll be happy when?' Meaning there are conditions you've identified before you'll allow yourself to be happy. Don't delay. Choose to be happy now. Be a happiness watcher today and observe people's response to your smiling face and also what happens to your day.

I take full responsibility for myself, my life and my happiness.

Today, I intend	I'm so happy and grateful
1.	1.
2.	2.
3.	3.

Day's End

I celebrate

I learned

I would change

*T*omorrow, I look forward to

I AM flourishing! I AM love, health, abundance, joy and success!

> "Go boldly where we have not allowed ourselves to go before and put ourselves first"
>
> –GILLIAN STEVENS

I feel good when

_____

_____

_____

_____

Inspired Action

BE A SELFIST! Be 'for' you today and make choices in your best interest. You'll spread so much joy when you do what makes you feel good. You'll be happier, have more energy for yourself and others and people will love to be around you. Win- Win. Aim to engage in something today that is for you, and feels good.

I love, accept and appreciate myself.

Today, I intend	I'm so happy and grateful
1.	1.
2.	2.
3.	3.

Day's End

I celebrate

I learned

I would change

*T*omorrow, I look forward to

I AM flourishing! I AM love, health, abundance, joy and success!

EXPLORE, TRANSFORM, FLOURISH COMPANION JOURNAL

> "Be thankful for what you have ; you'll end up having more. If you concentrate on what you don't have , you'll never, ever have enough."
>
> –OPRAH WINFREY

I'm abundant

_____

_____

_____

_____

Inspired Action

GRATITUDE! Begin the gratitude list at the back of the book and add to it regularly. An attitude of gratitude reflects an abundant mindset and creates the conditions for you to attract more to be thankful for. People have won the life lottery, they just don't act like they have. Be grateful instead and watch what happens.

I attract all I need and want with ease!

Today, I intend	I'm so happy and grateful
1.	1.
2.	2.
3.	3.

Day's End

I celebrate

I learned

I would change

*T*omorrow, I look forward to

I AM flourishing! I AM love, health, abundance, joy and success!

"The key to success is to start before you're ready."
—MARIE FORLEO

If I wasn't so scared

_____

_____

_____

_____

_____

Inspired Action

FEEL THE FEAR! Do it anyway. Naming what you're afraid of shines a light on the fear and reduces it's power over you. Take a deep breath, feel the fear in your body, thank it and then move in the direction of your dreams. Which area of your life do you want to start with? You've got this!

I trust myself to make fantastic decisions.

Today, I intend	I'm so happy and grateful
1.	1.
2.	2.
3.	3.

Day's End

I celebrate

I learned

I would change

*T*omorrow, I look forward to

I AM flourishing! I AM love, health, abundance, joy and success!

"Above all we must realize that each of us makes a difference with our life. Each of us impacts the world around us every single day. We have the choice to use the gift of our life to make the world a better place, or not to bother"

–JANE GODDALL

I care and my gifts are

_____

_____

_____

_____

Inspired Action

STAND! Did you know the balls of our feet carry 60% of our body's weight? Shift your weight more to your heels, align your feet, knees and hips and flex your knees. Connect to your root and ground yourself in the truth of who you are; a spark of the Divine. A stable, strong stance indicates alignment and confidence. You're here for a reason and not to be messed with!

I AM worthy of being loved, cherished and celebrated.

Today, I intend	*I'm so happy and grateful*
1.	1.
2.	2.
3.	3.

Day's End

I celebrate

I learned

I would change

*T*omorrow, I look forward to

I AM flourishing! I AM love, health, abundance, joy and success!

EXPLORE, TRANSFORM, FLOURISH COMPANION JOURNAL

The Life I'm Dreaming of....

Health

-
-
-
-
-

Happiness

-
-
-
-
-

Prosperity

-
-
-
-
-

Success

-
-
-
-
-

Relationships

-
-
-
-
-

Explore

" If you restore balance your own self, you will be contributing immensely to the healing of the world."

–DEEPAK CHOPRA

You Get What You Think About!

"Move forward with no second - guessing, no guilt trips, no hesitations. Your purpose is to recreate yourself anew in each moment."

–NEALE DONALD WALSCH

> "Women in particular need to keep an eye on their physical and mental health, because if we are scurrying to and from appointments and errands, we don't have a lot of time to take care of ourselves. We need to do a better job of putting ourselves higher on our own 'to do' list"
>
> –MICHELLE OBAMA

I 'should' on myself

_____

_____

_____

_____

Inspired Action

STEP UP! What could you do to prioritize your total well-being (physical, mental, emotional, spiritual and social)? Maybe there's something pressing that needs to be focused on first? Use the notes section to write down ideas and plan. It sticks if you enlist the support of your partner, family, co-workers so let them in on your plan. Have fun with this.

I value myself and what I need and want because I matter!

Today, I intend	I'm so happy and grateful
1.	1.
2.	2.
3.	3.

Day's End

I celebrate

I learned

I would change

*T*omorrow, I look forward to

I AM flourishing! I AM love, health, abundance, joy and success!

"Slow down and everything you are chasing will come around and catch you"

–JOHN DE PAOLA

*B*eing busy feels

Inspired Action

BREATHE! Observe how quickly you move in life and your eagerness to engage in life's dramas and gossip. Appreciate what slowing down feels like and take deep belly breaths. Breathing deeply soothes your nervous system, increases circulation and clarity and your body is energized. We move out of fight or flight and bonus, our metabolism and digestive system also benefit. When we slow down and focus on our lives surprisingly everything gets done with greater ease.

I choose to let everything in my life flow easily!

Today, I intend	I'm so happy and grateful
1.	1.
2.	2.
3.	3.

Day's End

I celebrate

I learned

I would change

*T*omorrow, I look forward to

I AM flourishing! I AM love, health, abundance, joy and success!

> "When you connect to the silence within you, that is when you can make sense of the disturbance going on around you."
>
> ## –STEPHEN RICHARDS

*I*n the quiet I
_____

_____

_____

_____

Inspired Action

VISUALIZE! Sit, eyes closed and imagine your ideal life. Using your dream list to prompt you write about that life in as much detail as possible, on your ' Ideal Life' page at the end of this section. Success is greatly enhanced when you write it down. Capture the essence of it with a word as a screen saver on your phone or computer. Read it and feel it here now, often!

My past has no power over me. I AM willing to learn, change and grow!

Today, I intend	I'm so happy and grateful
1.	1.
2.	2.
3.	3.

Day's End

I celebrate

I learned

I would change

*T*omorrow, I look forward to

I AM flourishing! I AM love, health, abundance, joy and success!

"We all know that the feminine values of well being, love, connection, inclusion and caring are critical to creating a world that works. But what if these feminine values are the keys to creating the life of your dreams?"

–KRIS CARR

*M*y superpower is

_____

_____

_____

_____

Inspired Action

INCLUSION! Women leaders are changing the world. Who's one step ahead of where you want to go? Some times it's difficult to ask for help as we feel less than or judged. Have the courage to do it anyway and ask them to help you with a professional or personal project. On the flip side, who could you support in achieving their dreams? Collaboration over competition. When one succeeds we all succeed.

I empower myself and all women in the world.

Today, I intend

1.
2.
3.

I'm so happy and grateful

1.
2.
3.

Day's End

I celebrate

I learned

I would change

*T*omorrow, I look forward to

I AM flourishing! I AM love, health, abundance, joy and success!

"The most important question to ask is, do you believe you live in a hostile or a friendly universe?"
–ALBERT EINSTEIN

I have faith in

_____

_____

_____

_____

Inspired Action

Positive! Observe your thoughts and words and particularly as you think and speak about yourself. Are your words more negative or positive? Would you speak to anyone else the way you speak to yourself? Make a commitment to be kinder to yourself and banish negative self talk. Believe the universe is conspiring for your good, always and act from this belief. Observe what you attract!

I live in a supportive universe. All is well in my world.

Today, I intend	*I'm so happy and grateful*
1.	1.
2.	2.
3.	3.

Day's End

I celebrate

I learned

I would change

*T*omorrow, I look forward to

I AM flourishing! I AM love, health, abundance, joy and success!

> "As the obstacles surface on your path of change, which inevitably they will, remember they are the way. Rub your hands together and go for it with excitement and enthusiasm"
>
> –GILLIAN STEVENS

The potential for change

_____

_____

_____

_____

Inspired Action

TRUST! Recognizing how we approach change enables us to shift and re-focus. Lean into any challenging situation with your breath first. Being calm and confident, out of the fight or flight response, you can consider all options and trust yourself to choose the best one. If you like, ask for a sign that nudges you in the right direction. Sometimes what we resist the most is the way!

I trust the process of life. I choose to have fun and make life a playful experience!

Today, I intend	I'm so happy and grateful
1.	1.
2.	2.
3.	3.

Day's End

I celebrate

I learned

I would change

*T*omorrow, I look forward to

I AM flourishing! I AM love, health, abundance, joy and success!

"Stress is an alarm clock that lets you know you are attached to something that is not true for you"
−BYRON KATIE

*W*hen I feel stressed

Inspired Action

NOURISH! Make it your intention today to shift from stressed to blessed by counting your blessings. Next, choose to feed your body, mind and spirit with energizing food, drink, thoughts and ideas. Consider taking a moment to bless whatever you put into your body. Remember you become what you think about, all day long so think happiness, health and gratitude.

I give myself permission to step away and take a break if I become stressed or anxious.

Today, I intend	I'm so happy and grateful
1.	1.
2.	2.
3.	3.

Day's End

I celebrate

I learned

I would change

*T*omorrow, I look forward to

I AM flourishing! I AM love, health, abundance, joy and success!

"What if we re-charged ourselves as often as we did our phones"

–UNKNOWN

*W*hat if?

Inspired Action

GOOD MORNING! When we approach our day with the intention of having a great day, the Universe conspires on our behalf. What do you want to accomplish today? Tackle your least favourable task first and avoid procrastination. You'll feel great and the other tasks will be completed with ease. Before bedtime do something that rejuvenates you; no if's, ands, or buts. That might even mean unplugging an hour before bed.

I celebrate all that is good/right in the world!

Today, I intend

1.
2.
3.

I'm so happy and grateful

1.
2.
3.

Day's End

I celebrate

I learned

I would change

Tomorrow, I look forward to

I AM flourishing! I AM love, health, abundance, joy and success!

EXPLORE, TRANSFORM, FLOURISH COMPANION JOURNAL

My Ideal Life

My ideal life...

GILLIAN STEVENS

"Love and compassion are necessities, not luxuries, without them humanity cannot survive."

–DALAI LAMA

Love Is Not An Action Word!

"I can assure you that the journey of following your deepest desires, of letting your heart lead you, is worth everything. It's the key to health, vibrancy and joy today, and at every age."

–DR. CHRISTIANE NORTHRUP

> "I have an everyday religion that works for me. Love yourself first and everything else falls into place"
> –LUCILLE BALL

I feel the love

_____

_____

_____

_____

Inspired Action

LOVE YOU! Look yourself, in the eyes, in the mirror and affirm out loud, with feeling "I love you!" Say this ten times today and for as many days as you can. The quality of our relationships is dependent on the one we have with ourselves so it does us good to love ourselves. The words you choose to say in your power mantra should ring true so start where you are. Big hug!

I (am willing to) love and accept everything about me!

Today, I intend

1.
2.
3.

I'm so happy and grateful

1.
2.
3.

Day's End

I celebrate

I learned

I would change

*T*omorrow, I look forward to

I AM flourishing! I AM love, health, abundance, joy and success!

> "Whenever you meet anyone, remember they are going through a great war"
>
> −RALPH WALDO EMERSON

*M*y triggers are

_____

_____

_____

_____

Inspired Action

MAKE MY DAY! Everything is either love or a call for love. Pause before reacting when you're triggered by what someone says or does. Take the high road and give them the benefit of the doubt. We don't know what kind of a day they're having, and we also have a perception based on our previous experiences. Pausing and reflecting allows for a calm, sensitive response.

I open my heart to all beings on the planet!

Today, I intend	I'm so happy and grateful
1.	1.
2.	2.
3.	3.

Day's End

I celebrate

I learned

I would change

*T*omorrow, I look forward to

I AM flourishing! I AM love, health, abundance, joy and success!

> "Love is what we are born with. Fear is what we learn. The spiritual journey is the unlearning of fear and prejudices and the acceptance of love back in our hearts"
>
> —MARIANNE WILLIAMSON

My childhood taught me

_____

_____

_____

_____

Inspired Action

HOW DO I LOVE THEE? What do you love about yourself? Use the page, "Ya, I'm that good! " at the back of the book and list everything you love about you. What you're proud of. What makes you unique. Don't be shy! Pssst... use this as your feel good, 'go to' list to refer to when you're not having a great day.

I invite love into my life. I AM lovable and able to give and receive unconditional love!

Today, I intend	*I'm so happy and grateful*
1.	1.
2.	2.
3.	3.

Day's End

I celebrate

I learned

I would change

*T*omorrow, I look forward to

I AM flourishing! I AM love, health, abundance, joy and success!

> "It's impossible." said pride.
> "It's risky." said experience.
> "It's pointless." said reason.
> "Give it a try." whispered the heart.
>
> —UNKNOWN

Relationships take courage

_____

_____

_____

_____

Inspired Action

SECRET, SECRET! Did you know the root word of courage is 'coeur' meaning heart? We're all wounded and it takes courage to follow our heart and be love in action however it's what you don't bring to a relationship that's missing. Take a step toward attracting more love into your life by acting as if you're in love. That's the ticket, both in a relationship and in attracting a relationship. Make some notes about what you want in a partner and then be the match for that person.

I choose to trust my inner guidance and know my heart will never steer me wrong!

Today, I intend	I'm so happy and grateful
1.	1.
2.	2.
3.	3.

Day's End

I celebrate

I learned

I would change

*T*omorrow, I look forward to

I AM flourishing! I AM love, health, abundance, joy and success!

"You aren't a rehab. It is not your job to fix everyone"
–UNKNOWN

I can't fix

_____

_____

_____

_____

Inspired Action

LET GO AND LET GOD! It feels good to look after others however sometimes we overstep and enable to reduce our fear and pain. In a society where addiction is rampant, codependency traits of caretaking can be confused with caregiving. If this resonates with you, perhaps seek a recovery group and / or online resources. In the meantime seek support, spiritual and emotional, to detach from unhealthy behaviours.

God grant me the serenity to accept the things I cannot change, the courage to change the things I can, and the wisdom to know the difference!

Today, I intend	*I'm so happy and grateful*
1.	1.
2.	2.
3.	3.

Day's End

I celebrate

I learned

I would change

*T*omorrow, I look forward to

I AM flourishing! I AM love, health, abundance, joy and success!

> "Let today be the day you love yourself enough to no longer just dream of a better life; let it be the day you act on it"

—STEVE MARABOLI

I love myself enough

_____

_____

_____

_____

Inspired Action

S*AY* '*YES*'*!* Life can be serious and full of responsibility. Today happily take some action toward living your ideal life. Do something for fun. You deserve it! Saying 'yes' to you and what you desire aligns your thoughts, beliefs and actions and gets you going in the right direction.

Today I am aware of my dreams and I intend to pursue them!

Today, I intend

1.

2.

3.

I'm so happy and grateful

1.

2.

3.

Day's End

I celebrate

I learned

I would change

Tomorrow, I look forward to

I AM flourishing! I AM love, health, abundance, joy and success!

> "We burn out not because we don't care but because we don't grieve. We burn out because we allowed our hearts to become so filled with loss that we have no room left to care"

–DR. RACHEL REMEN

I feel sad

_____

_____

_____

_____

Inspired Action

Joy! We can't be sad, broke, sick enough to help someone else. Read that again! There is nothing to be ashamed of or to feel guilty for living the good life. Today choose joy and seek opportunities to share your passions with others, to feel good, to inspire and elevate your mood and day. You'll be adding to the energy in the world so shine your light.

I release old habits that are limiting my potential!

Today, I intend

1.
2.
3.

I'm so happy and grateful

1.
2.
3.

Day's End

I celebrate

I learned

I would change

*T*omorrow, I look forward to

I AM flourishing! I AM love, health, abundance, joy and success!

> "First and foremost, if we maintain healthy emotional boundaries and direct love and kindness inwards, we are taking care of ourselves, and, secondly, we are giving a subliminal message to others about how we wish to be treated. People tend to subconsciously treat us how we treat ourselves"

–CHRISTOPHER DINES

I express love and kindness

_____

_____

_____

_____

Inspired Action

RAK! Pay it forward with a random act of kindness. Do it playfully and without needing the acknowledgement or thank you. Before you do for someone else, treat yourself with some loving kindness. Is there a body treatment you would relish? We teach people how to treat us so be clear and concise in your interactions today. That is love!

I stand up for myself by saying how I truly feel with kindness!

Today, I intend

1.

2.

3.

I'm so happy and grateful

1.

2.

3.

Day's End

I celebrate

I learned

I would change

*T*omorrow, I look forward to

I AM flourishing! I AM love, health, abundance, joy and success!

"*No one is you. That is your superpower.*"
–JEN SINCERO

Stuck In a Rut, Or Are You...

*"Our stories hold unique inspiration
for one another."*
–LAILAH GIFTY AKITA

"Please stop destroying what is left of your heart by constantly thinking about the things that have broken you"

—NIKITA GILL

*S*ilver linings and lessons

Inspired Action

FLOURISH! By now you've learned and accomplished a great deal. Take the lesson from those emotionally painful times and even in those periods of struggle, you know there has been a silver lining. Use these successes to alleviate self doubt in challenging times. Now, stop defining yourself by your story and past events. Your cells are always replenishing so you're not even the same person, literally!

I AM radiating positive energy and this is my time to shine!

Today, I intend

1.

2.

3.

I'm so happy and grateful

1.

2.

3.

Day's End

I celebrate

I learned

I would change

*T*omorrow, I look forward to

I AM flourishing! I AM love, health, abundance, joy and success!

> "When you complain, you make yourself a victim. Leave a situation, change the situation or accept it. All else is madness."
>
> —ECKHART TOLLE

I release and let go

_____

_____

_____

_____

Inspired Action

VICTOR! Create a life graph of your up's and down's and list what you learned from each. Use some pages at the back of the book, coloured pens and have some fun. You might be surprised when you realize the seemingly painful experiences were catalysts to better! Take some time with this, no rush, and be open to the realizations.

Nothing is as great as my own personal power! I have the power to create a flourishing life.

Today, I intend	I'm so happy and grateful
1.	1.
2.	2.
3.	3.

Day's End

I celebrate

I learned

I would change

*T*omorrow, I look forward to

I AM flourishing! I AM love, health, abundance, joy and success!

"No matter how you feel, get up, dress up, show up and never give up"

–REGINA BRETT

I just can't
_____

_____

_____

_____

Inspired Action

IT'S OK! Some days this quote provides just the prod you need and other days it's impossible to get going. Give yourself permission to cocoon and take care of you. It's healthy to do what's necessary to support yourself in times of loss, sorrow, fatigue, disappointment etc. When you do this, you also encourage others, by your actions, to make the same choice for personal well-being.

I feel _____ and it's OK for me to take the time to feel my feelings.

Today, I intend   *I'm so happy and grateful*

1.   1.

2.   2.

3.   3.

Day's End

I celebrate

I learned

I would change

*T*omorrow, I look forward to

I AM flourishing! I AM love, health, abundance, joy and success!

"We have all been placed on this earth to discover our own path, and we will never be happy if we live someone else's idea of life"

–JAMES VAN PRAGH

*M*y experiences help

_____

_____

_____

_____

Inspired Action

SHARE! Is there an individual, an organization, a community who could benefit from your wisdom? Reach out and offer to share, to speak or post a solution to a problem you faced on social media. Animals are unconditional love. Spend time loving up your pet or consider fostering / adopting a rescue dog or cat. If that's not possible maybe volunteer at a shelter? Love is love.

I AM meant to be here and to impact the world in profound ways!

Today, I intend	I'm so happy and grateful
1.	1.
2.	2.
3.	3.

Day's End

I celebrate

I learned

I would change

*T*omorrow, I look forward to

I AM flourishing! I AM love, health, abundance, joy and success!

"Life begins at the end of your comfort zone. So if you're feeling uncomfortable right now, know that the change taking place in your life is a beginning not an ending"

−NEALE DONALD WALSCH

I'm beginning

_____

_____

_____

_____

Inspired Action

CHANGE! What change are you so very proud of? Add it to the "Ya, I'm that good" list! Feeling good about oneself is an inside job and you don't need anyone else's approval or accolades. You have overcome obstacles, adapted and you alone know how difficult it was. Celebrate cos you're a rockstar! Treat yourself as one. Give some thought to what that looks like.

I AM worthy and deserve all the incredible opportunities coming to me!

Today, I intend	I'm so happy and grateful
1.	1.
2.	2.
3.	3.

Day's End

I celebrate

I learned

I would change

*T*omorrow, I look forward to

I AM flourishing! I AM love, health, abundance, joy and success!

"To be happy you have to make peace with your past, love the present and feel so excited about the future"
—MARISA PEERS

I feel peace

___

___

___

___

Inspired Action

SHINE! How would those close to you positively describe you? Focus on those words today and allow your body and behaviour to express that pride and delight in accepting who you are. Scientific studies confirm that how we speak to water and plants impacts their biology. Since we are 75% water doesn't it make sense that how we speak to ourselves can positively or negatively impact our wellbeing? Be conscious.

I AM always evolving and becoming the best version of myself!

Today, I intend

1.

2.

3.

I'm so happy and grateful

1.

2.

3.

Day's End

I celebrate

I learned

I would change

*T*omorrow, I look forward to

I AM flourishing! I AM love, health, abundance, joy and success!

"If you have been brutally broken but still have the courage to be gentle to other living things, then you're a badass with the heart of an angel"

–KEANU REEVES

I'm a badass

_____

_____

_____

_____

_____

Inspired Action

SERVICE! Be proud of your resiliency. Make a difference in the world by sharing your story. The world needs your attitude, your strength and your story to inspire others. Consider the best way to be of service; a book, a talk, one on one, or in a new career direction. Set the intention that you're "attracting opportunities to be of service now" and see what happens.

I AM grateful for my past and now I choose to engage fully in this present moment.

Today, I intend	I'm so happy and grateful
1.	1.
2.	2.
3.	3.

Day's End

I celebrate

I learned

I would change

*T*omorrow, I look forward to

I AM flourishing! I AM love, health, abundance, joy and success!

"We have to look for the better and not hold out for perfection"

–KATHY FRESTON

I forgive myself (others) for ....

....

....

....

Inspired Action

NEW LIGHT! Come clean and admit what you don't like about yourself. Where did you get those beliefs? The thoughts we think repeatedly become our beliefs and when we really look at them, we realize they're not true. With some lightness, consider what you've come to believe about yourself and record them on the 'Shift Happens' page at the end of this section. Opposite the not so nice statements write an empowering statement that feels true.

I forgive myself for what I didn't know and I'm grateful I know better!

Today, I intend	I'm so happy and grateful
1.	1.
2.	2.
3.	3.

Day's End

I celebrate

I learned

I would change

*T*omorrow, I look forward to

I AM flourishing! I AM love, health, abundance, joy and success!

Shift Happens

Disempowered thought:

Ex: I don't speak up in front of others

My empowered statement:

I thoughtfully take my time so as to speak effectively

GILLIAN STEVENS

Transform

"To me, finding my faith, right now where I'm at, is putting all my trust in something bigger than myself and living for something bigger than myself and trying to do that through service."

—NOOR TAGOURI

Dancing As Fast As You Can

"Flock with others who are truly,
madly and deeply in love with life."
–IAN LAWTON

EXPLORE, TRANSFORM, FLOURISH COMPANION JOURNAL

> "The most talented thought provoking game changing people are never normal"
>
> –RICHARD BRANSON

I'm glad I'm not normal

_____

_____

_____

_____

Inspired Action

GOOD, BAD, UGLY! We're an average of the five people we associate with the most. What traits do you have in common? Any you would like to change? What do you admire? Use the notes pages at the back and also add to other journal lists what you have discovered. You could design your own list as well?

I use my skills, experiences and talent to fulfil my life's purpose!

Today, I intend	I'm so happy and grateful
1.	1.
2.	2.
3.	3.

Day's End

I celebrate

I learned

I would change

*T*omorrow, I look forward to

I AM flourishing! I AM love, health, abundance, joy and success!

"Move it, stretch it, nourish it, hydrate it. Pay attention. The better our bodies feel the happier and more productive we are"

–JEN SINCERO

I feel better when

_____

_____

_____

_____

Inspired Action

MOVE AND REST! Notice the use of the word 'move' instead of 'workout'. There's much joy in movement and workout implies another meaning completely. Move cos it feels good not because you deny yourself a treat unless you've worked out. Balance your day's activity with rest and sleep. Our bodies and brains rejuvenate with sleep so do what you can to get your optimal amount.

My body vibrates with health and energy!

Today, I intend

1.

2.

3.

I'm so happy and grateful

1.

2.

3.

Day's End

I celebrate

I learned

I would change

*T*omorrow, I look forward to

I AM flourishing! I AM love, health, abundance, joy and success!

"The most dangerous thing you can do in life is play it safe"

–CASEY NEISTAT

I play safe when

_____

_____

_____

_____

Inspired Action

VIBE! Energy attracts like energy aka your vibe tribe and to take risks we need to feel safe. Do you have a cheerleader in your vibe tribe who's always there for you? If so enlist their support in doing something that pushes you a bit out of your comfort zone. We're either growing or we're dying. Are you your own cheerleader? Both are essential. Reach out and start that connection.

I choose to let go relationships that no longer support me!

Today, I intend

1.
2.
3.

I'm so happy and grateful

1.
2.
3.

Day's End

I celebrate

I learned

I would change

*T*omorrow, I look forward to

I AM flourishing! I AM love, health, abundance, joy and success!

EXPLORE, TRANSFORM, FLOURISH COMPANION JOURNAL

"As you move along in life, adopt some things, adapt some, drop some and have some fun doing your adapting, adopting and dropping"

–CARI CORBETT-OWEN

What will I adopt, adapt, drop?

_____

_____

_____

_____

Inspired Action

PLAY! Laugh and have some fun as you face your responsibilities and consider where you can simplify your life. It's said a cluttered house reflects a cluttered mind so what steps can you take to declutter and organize? Marie Kondo's book: The Japanese Art of Decluttering and Organizing could be a good resource. Start to declutter today.

I give myself permission to step away, take a break from life and play!

Today, I intend	I'm so happy and grateful
1.	1.
2.	2.
3.	3.

Day's End

I celebrate

I learned

I would change

*T*omorrow, I look forward to

I AM flourishing! I AM love, health, abundance, joy and success!

> "The secret to leadership is simple. Do what you believe. Paint a picture of the future. Go there. People will follow"
>
> ## –SETH GODIN

I'm good at

_____

_____

_____

_____

Inspired Action

INSPIRATION! Who and what inspires you? Do you have anything in common? Is there someone in your close proximity who could be part of your vibe tribe? Jot your ideas down on the "What Inspires Me" page at the back of the book. Add to it when you stumble onto something/ someone really great.

I AM doing my best to make this world a safe and loving place for all of us!

Today, I intend	I'm so happy and grateful
1.	1.
2.	2.
3.	3.

Day's End

I celebrate

I learned

I would change

*T*omorrow, I look forward to

I AM flourishing! I AM love, health, abundance, joy and success!

> "The natural state of things is to disorganize and decay, and that will happen to your love relationships if you don't consciously put energy back into the system"
>
> –JON BUTCHER

*Y*ou make me feel

_____

_____

_____

_____

_____

Inspired Action

SHOW THEM! How do you spend quality time with those you love? Enlist their help in planning an occasion to engage in what you enjoy. It might be with your partner, your family, your children or close friends. We never know when we'll leave this physical existence so schedule it now and make it happen, together!

I allow myself to be loved fully!

Today, I intend

1.
2.
3.

I'm so happy and grateful

1.
2.
3.

Day's End

I celebrate

I learned

I would change

*T*omorrow, I look forward to

I AM flourishing! I AM love, health, abundance, joy and success!

> *"If you want to create change, you have to do it from a level of energy greater than guilt, greater than pain, greater than fear, greater than anger, greater than shame and greater than unworthiness"*

–DR. JOE DISPENZA

That has me thinking

_____
_____
_____
_____
_____

Inspired Action

ENERGY! It's our energy before we even speak our words that determines how someone will respond to us. Our feelings, or emotions make up that energetic signature so be aware how you feel and do what you can to shift your energetic state to positively impact your interaction. Learn about shifting your state. You will create greater success in all areas of your life.

I AM safe in my relationships and can express who I truly am!

Today, I intend	I'm so happy and grateful
1.	1.
2.	2.
3.	3.

Day's End

I celebrate

I learned

I would change

*T*omorrow, I look forward to

I AM flourishing! I AM love, health, abundance, joy and success!

EXPLORE, TRANSFORM, FLOURISH COMPANION JOURNAL

"Do what you can, with what you have, where you are"
–THEODORE ROOSEVELT

*B*eing gentle

Inspired Action

*T*OGETHER! Sometimes it's easier to accept others than accept ourselves. Today, be easy on yourself; speak gently, take it slower, acknowledge your humanness and do something just for you! Some days are harder than others and you deserve a break. Your actions inspire those around you, and our children learn by watching what we do.

Rest, Release, Replenish. I'm taking care of me!

Today, I intend	*I'm so happy and grateful*
1.	1.
2.	2.
3.	3.

Day's End

I celebrate

I learned

I would change

*T*omorrow, I look forward to

I AM flourishing! I AM love, health, abundance, joy and success!

"Most human beings underestimate just how powerful their thoughts are in creating the world around them."
—VISHEN LAKHIANI

Starting With The (Wo)Man in The Mirror

"Life is a series of near misses. But a lot of what we ascribe to luck is not luck at all. It's seizing the day and accepting responsibility for our future."
–HOWARD SCHULTZ

> "You are enough. Not because you did or said or thought or bought or became or created something special, but because you always were"
> —MARISA PEER

I'm enough
_____
_____
_____
_____

Inspired Action

WORTH! Our self worth is tied to our net worth. Bump your self worth by always affirming your "enoughness". Watch the YouTube video entitled "The Biggest Disease Facing Humanity - I am enough" for inspiration. List any other resources you come across on your 'What Inspires me' page. If you haven't continued saying 'I love you' in the mirror, consider beginning that again.

I AM extremely capable and I attract massive amounts of happiness, success and abundance!

Today, I intend	I'm so happy and grateful
1.	1.
2.	2.
3.	3.

Day's End

I celebrate

I learned

I would change

*T*omorrow, I look forward to

I AM flourishing! I AM love, health, abundance, joy and success!

> "Work is a rubber ball. If you drop it, it will bounce back. The other four balls -family, health, friends, integrity- are made of glass. If you drop one of these, it will be irrevocably scuffed, nicked, perhaps even shattered"
>
> —GARY W KELLER

My work-life balance

_____

_____

_____

_____

Inspired Action

BELIEVE! Today, make a conscious effort to weed out the beliefs that aren't in alignment with who you want to be. Use the page 'I AM Unlimited' at the end of this section to write down your beliefs and then shift them from limited to unlimited following the example. Most of our beliefs about work, family, money, health etc are inherited. Becoming aware of our beliefs is ongoing so no rush to complete this.

I AM limitless.
I AM open to more good than I can imagine!

Today, I intend	*I'm so happy and grateful*
1.	1.
2.	2.
3.	3.

Day's End

I celebrate

I learned

I would change

*T*omorrow, I look forward to

I AM flourishing! I AM love, health, abundance, joy and success!

> "A balance of giving and receiving is essential to keeping your energy, mood and motivation at a consistently high level"
> —DOREEN VIRTUE

I struggle with receiving

_____

_____

_____

_____

Inspired Action

MORNING! Develop a 15 minute ritual that feeds your body, mind and soul and commit to it for one week. By giving to ourselves, it's good practice setting personal boundaries and in asking and receiving from others. After a week, tweak your routine. Observe how starting your day this way affects your energy, mood, motivation and success.

I embrace the day, vibrating with positive creative energy. I AM unstoppable!

Today, I intend	I'm so happy and grateful
1.	1.
2.	2.
3.	3.

Day's End

I celebrate

I learned

I would change

*T*omorrow, I look forward to

I AM flourishing! I AM love, health, abundance, joy and success!

"If today were the last day of my life, would I want to do what I'm about to do today?"
—STEVE JOBS

I would

_____

_____

_____

_____

Inspired Action

FREEDOM! So many Brules (BS rules) in life. Who made them anyway? Call in sick, not for illness but for wellness. Take a longer lunch, do something out of the ordinary, be a little rebellious and thoroughly enjoy it. Dare you! And so proud of you!

I AM a fun loving, carefree spirit

Today, I intend

1.
2.
3.

I'm so happy and grateful

1.
2.
3.

Day's End

I celebrate

I learned

I would change

*T*omorrow, I look forward to

I AM flourishing! I AM love, health, abundance, joy and success!

> "When you slow down, step back a moment and put things in perspective, you can then move on with more efficiency. It only takes a moment to adapt and control how you respond"

–DOC CHILDRE

I have regrets

_____

_____

_____

_____

Inspired Action

CHALLENGE! The challenge is to make choices that align with your core values and that might ruffle some feathers. A life altering choice, like going plant based, might create some resistance with your partner or family members. Do it anyway! Keep making conscious choices in how you spend your money and your time to reflect your values.

*I take daily action in things that matter to me.
What someone thinks of me is none of my business!*

Today, I intend

1.
2.
3.

I'm so happy and grateful

1.
2.
3.

Day's End

I celebrate

I learned

I would change

*T*omorrow, I look forward to

I AM flourishing! I AM love, health, abundance, joy and success!

"When you do not seek or need external approval, you are at your most powerful"

–CAROLINE MYSS

I don't care what people think

_____

_____

_____

_____

Inspired Action

GRIT! Passion and perseverance. What's that one soulful thing you're afraid to try for fear of failure and humiliation and yet you know it will absolutely change your life? As you continue to evolve your confidence is growing. Grit your teeth, call on your vibe tribe and your cheerleader and go for it!

I now release my need for approval and self doubt. I have the desire and grit to achieve whatever I want!

Today, I intend	I'm so happy and grateful
1.	1.
2.	2.
3.	3.

Day's End

I celebrate

I learned

I would change

*T*omorrow, I look forward to

I AM flourishing! I AM love, health, abundance, joy and success!

> "What if we were taught from a very early age that wealth, purpose and prosperity are what eliminate poverty and human suffering? Money is not some sort of spiritual defect but the highest form of contribution?"
>
> —JON BUTCHER

If I had unlimited money I would

_____

_____

_____

_____

Inspired Action

TEACH! To teach is to demonstrate. Consider what you say and do relative to this quote. What are you teaching about caring and sharing, how to treat others and your beliefs about money? Make one noticeable change that shifts how you treat money and others. Maybe make a plan to donate regularly. The world thanks you!

I AM abundant. I attract exactly what I need, when I need it.

Today, I intend	I'm so happy and grateful
1.	1.
2.	2.
3.	3.

Day's End

I celebrate

I learned

I would change

*T*omorrow, I look forward to

I AM flourishing! I AM love, health, abundance, joy and success!

> "Nobody cares how much you know until they know how much you care"
> –THEODORE ROOSEVELT

*T*he world needs

_____

_____

_____

_____

Inspired Action

THE 4 C's! We often didn't Cause it, nor can we Control, Cure or Change it. Withdrawing our energy by not reacting, not resisting to an intense situation, and remaining as neutral as possible, we're able to access the power of our mind. Find a tool that centres you and helps you find peace. We need that!

I AM aware that everything and everyone in the Universe is connected!

Today, I intend	*I'm so happy and grateful*
1.	1.
2.	2.
3.	3.

Day's End

I celebrate

I learned

I would change

*T*omorrow, I look forward to

I AM flourishing! I AM love, health, abundance, joy and success!

I AM Unlimited

Limiting Beliefs	Unlimited Thinking
Our bodies go downhill as we age.	My health reflects how I think about and treat my body.

GILLIAN STEVENS

"We're here to put a dent in the universe otherwise why else be here?"

−STEVE JOBS

Don't Die With Your Music Still Inside You

"Be the hero in your own movie. Pretend that your life was a movie and it started now. What would the hero do? What would the person that you respect do? What would the person you admire, and inspires you do? Do that."

–JOE ROGAN

> "You must not lose faith in humanity. Humanity is like an ocean; if a few drops of the ocean are dirty, the ocean doesn't become dirty"
>
> —GANDHI

*W*itnessing man's inhumanity

_____

_____

_____

_____

Inspired Action

REVERENCE! Where's that place that connects you to God/Spirit? Do you commune with your higher self in nature; in water, walking in the woods, leaning against a tree? Make that connection a priority either when you wake, or before the day is done. Breathe deeply as a way to connect to your Higher Self in addition to creating greater health and well-being.

I surround myself with people who bring out the best in me!

Today, I intend	I'm so happy and grateful
1.	1.
2.	2.
3.	3.

Day's End

I celebrate

I learned

I would change

*T*omorrow, I look forward to

I AM flourishing! I AM love, health, abundance, joy and success!

> "I challenge you to make your life a masterpiece. I challenge you to join the ranks of those people who live what they teach, who walk their talk"
>
> –TONY ROBBINS

A challenge I'm facing

Inspired Action

TWEAK! Review your ideal life page and consider what's missing. You're consistently changing now so your life might need some adaptation. What could you do more or less of? Take another step toward upgrading your life and don't be shy. You've been working that faith muscle. Today, go big or go home as they say!

I'm so grateful! I act as if I already have everything I want in my life and in doing so I attract more to be grateful for!

Today, I intend	*I'm so happy and grateful*
1.	1.
2.	2.
3.	3.

Day's End

I celebrate

I learned

I would change

*T*omorrow, I look forward to

I AM flourishing! I AM love, health, abundance, joy and success!

> "One of the realities of grief and loss is that the rest of the world seems to keep on going forward while we feel we have been stopped in our tracks"
>
> ## –DR. ALAN WOLFELT

I feel stuck when

___

Inspired Action

STUCK! Underneath anger and depression lies hurt and sadness. Sometimes we're hanging on to connections, stories and circumstances that keep us stuck. Repeating the Ho'oponopono prayer while thinking of others and troubling circumstances is helpful in times of confusion and stuckness. "I'm sorry. Please forgive me. Thank you. I Love you." Try it! Jot down any prayers that provide you comfort in the notes section at the back of the book.

As I forgive myself, it becomes easier to forgive others!

Today, I intend	*I'm so happy and grateful*
1.	1.
2.	2.
3.	3.

Day's End

I celebrate

I learned

I would change

*T*omorrow, I look forward to

I AM flourishing! I AM love, health, abundance, joy and success!

"Go find your joy. Whatever this is, go find your joy. Are you going to have a good day, or are you going to have a great day? Because it's completely up to you"

–SANDRA BULLOCK

*J*oy
_____
_____
_____
_____

Inspired Action

INTENTION! You've been setting daily intentions so consider setting intentions for the week, the month, the year. Reflect on your lists, and use your imagination. Choose accomplishments that make a difference and word them as intentions. You don't have to know the 'how'. Write them out, in present tense and place them where you can see them every day. Feel them as done!

I choose to be authentic and fully me even if it requires me to be vulnerable and challenge myself!

Today, I intend	I'm so happy and grateful
1.	1.
2.	2.
3.	3.

Day's End

I celebrate

I learned

I would change

*T*omorrow, I look forward to

I AM flourishing! I AM love, health, abundance, joy and success!

> "We do not see the world as the world is we see the world as we are"
> —STEPHEN COVEY

I see the world
_____
_____
_____
_____

Inspired Action

EVERYTHING IS FIGUREOUTABLE! Meditation slows us down, helping us achieve focus and gain clarity and when we relax the answer makes itself known. No pressure, just experiment with any meditative practice and observe the change, in you, and how you're much more present. Everything really is figureoutable, and it doesn't have to be you doing the figuring. Tap in.

My outer world is a reflection of my inner world. I AM calm and trust my soul's guidance!

Today, I intend

1.
2.
3.

I'm so happy and grateful

1.
2.
3.

Day's End

I celebrate

I learned

I would change

*T*omorrow, I look forward to

I AM flourishing! I AM love, health, abundance, joy and success!

"The absence of ordinary pleasures may take an even greater toll on our health than stress. So, trade frowns for smiles. Turn on your imagination. Be different. Tap into your humour and eat dessert first"

–LORETTA LAROCHE

It's getting easier to

_____

_____

_____

_____

Inspired Action

PRAY! Surrender any concerns you have to the power greater than you. Once you have given them over, trust and have faith your prayer is answered. Exercise that faith muscle and at the same time enjoy life and eat dessert first! Really. At the end of this section there's a formula for how to write affirmative prayer.

I AM happy! I AM me! I AM not alone!

Today, I intend

1.
2.
3.

I'm so happy and grateful

1.
2.
3.

Day's End

I celebrate

I learned

I would change

*T*omorrow, I look forward to

I AM flourishing! I AM love, health, abundance, joy and success!

EXPLORE, TRANSFORM, FLOURISH COMPANION JOURNAL

"You have resources yet to be unleashed. Make bold, courageous choices. Live as though you have the power to change the world- because you do"

– CAROLINE MYSS

*M*y life has transformed

_____

_____

_____

_____

Inspired Action

PURPOSE! Believe in your power to make a difference. You're here for a reason. Your greatest challenge was life transforming and is the inspiration and hope for others in transforming their lives. That's living your purpose. Pop the bubbly and celebrate how amazing you are! (Need a reminder? Read your "Ya, I'm that good" page, and even add to it)

I AM in charge of my life! I say 'yes' to life and life says 'yes' to me!

Today, I intend	*I'm so happy and grateful*
1.	1.
2.	2.
3.	3.

Day's End

I celebrate

I learned

I would change

*T*omorrow, I look forward to

I AM flourishing! I AM love, health, abundance, joy and success!

"Hello, you're looking gorgeous today!"

I'm on top of my game

Inspired Action

RADIANCE! You're radiant when you feel good, feel successful and express health. Your energy positively impacts others when you move through your day exuding self confidence and knowing your worth. You'll be noticed, as you should be and draw people and love toward you! Own your beauty and power today.

I feel sexy and desirable! I AM beautiful inside and out!

Today, I intend	*I'm so happy and grateful*
1.	1.
2.	2.
3.	3.

Day's End

I celebrate

I learned

I would change

*T*omorrow, I look forward to

I AM flourishing! I AM love, health, abundance, joy and success!

Prayer Works!

Use when you are faced with a challenge or about a change you would like to see.

Use this to be happier, more fulfilled and manifest what you would like in your life.

Affirmative prayer is about claiming it now so speak in present tense as if it is done, now.

*Affirmative prayer based on Spiritual Mind Treatment format.

1. *Imagine what you want. Say it outloud. For example: I speak these words for ......*

2. *Acknowledging God, Spirit, Source and feeling the truth of your belief in something greater than you. For example: I recognize God is a loving presence that flows through and around every living person and thing......*

3. *Unifying. This step is about recognizing you are a part of this benevolent presence. For example: I am connected to this Source of good, love and wisdom as a spark of the Divine......*

4. *Claiming. State your desire in present tense, as truth. For example: I am happy and healthy. I attract abundance in all areas of my life....*

5. *Feeling. Imagine how you will feel when you receive what you want. Feel the experience. Feelings intensify your claim and add speed to it's manifestation in your life.*

6. *Gratitude. I am so happy and grateful now that I.......*

7. *Release. I release and let go. Or All is well. Or Amen.*

Flourish

"Knowing one self comes from attending with compassionate curiosity to what is happening."

−GABOR MATE

All Is Well

"Live with intention. Walk to the edge. Listen hard. Practice wellness. Play with abandon. Laugh. Choose with no regret. Appreciate your friends. Continue to learn. Do what you love. Live as if this is all there is."
—MARY ANNE RADMACHER

> "The Japanese term 'wabi sabi' is the appreciation for the imperfections in yourself and others. It's about accepting who we are - imperfect, unfinished and mortal- and through the passage of time, accepting and appreciating where we've been damaged and the beauty and value of those experiences"
>
> —GILLIAN STEVENS

I love this idea

_____

_____

_____

_____

Inspired Action

WABI SABI! Appreciate your own beauty, see the beauty in others and in life itself. There's no rush to complete anything. No need to be perfect. Move through your day unencumbered by your 'to do' list and feel the freedom of that choice today. Be in the ease and flow of life. By now this is easier?

I'm excited about everything because even more good is on it's way to me!

Today, I intend	I'm so happy and grateful
1.	1.
2.	2.
3.	3.

Day's End

I celebrate

I learned

I would change

*T*omorrow, I look forward to

I AM flourishing! I AM love, health, abundance, joy and success!

"Our deepest fear is not that we are inadequate. Our deepest fear is that we are powerful beyond measure. It is our light, not our darkness, that most frightens us"

—MARIANNE WILLIAMSON

What lights me up

_____

_____

_____

_____

Inspired Action

GENEROSITY! Be generous of spirit. Reserve judgement of yourself and others and choose to see the love everywhere and in everyone, including yourself. Believe the universe is conspiring for your good and that everyone is doing the best they can. Today, tell someone how much their presence in your life means to you.

I radiate a positive vibrating energy!

Today, I intend	I'm so happy and grateful
1.	1.
2.	2.
3.	3.

Day's End

I celebrate

I learned

I would change

*T*omorrow, I look forward to

I AM flourishing! I AM love, health, abundance, joy and success!

> *"Our survival as a species depends on our ability to recognize that our well being and the well being of others are in fact one and the same"*
> — MARSHALL B ROSENBERG

If I had a magic wand

_____

_____

_____

_____

Inspired Action

INFLUENCE! What's one cause that keeps you up at night? Reach out and offer your help, inspiration, services, time to a local or global cause that is near and dear to your heart. It feels great to help each other, animals and our planet and you have the power to make a difference.

I don't wait for the world to give me what I want. I give myself what I need and I give the world what I long to see.

Today, I intend	I'm so happy and grateful
1.	1.
2.	2.
3.	3.

Day's End

I celebrate

I learned

I would change

*T*omorrow, I look forward to

I AM flourishing! I AM love, health, abundance, joy and success!

"You need messiness and magic, serendipity and insanity. Creativity comes from time off and time out"
–TIMOTHY EGAN

I dare to

_____

_____

_____

_____

Inspired Action

SERENDIPITY! The unexpected happens when we're least expecting it and having fun! Taking a break from the grind and doing something crazy will attract what you are seeking. We've been taught to believe nothing without hard work. Choose to do it differently and allow what you want to come to you by taking it easy and loosening your hold on what you want. Trust that!

I'm wild and carefree and just plain fun to be around!

Today, I intend	I'm so happy and grateful
1.	1.
2.	2.
3.	3.

Day's End

I celebrate

I learned

I would change

*T*omorrow, I look forward to

I AM flourishing! I AM love, health, abundance, joy and success!

"Getting out of bed in the morning with a reason for living is as important as sunshine, fresh water and all the other things that help people live a long time"

—BEN GREENFIELD

I live for
_____
_____
_____
_____

Inspired Action

BLISS! Nobody gets out of here alive so focus on what you *CAN* do and look for solutions rather than problems. If you're facing a challenge, health or otherwise, do what you can to shift your perception. If you need some support consider an accountability partner who will help you stay committed to your new way of thinking. All the while, choose to believe in miracles. You'll inspire others.

I AM alive right now and I choose to engage fully and enthusiastically in my life!

Today, I intend	I'm so happy and grateful
1.	1.
2.	2.
3.	3.

Day's End

I celebrate

I learned

I would change

*T*omorrow, I look forward to

I AM flourishing! I AM love, health, abundance, joy and success!

> "You are learning too much, remembering too much, trying too hard... relax a little bit, give life a chance to flow its own way, unassisted by your mind and effort"
>
> –MOOJI

I've a hard time saying 'no'

_____

_____

_____

_____

Inspired Action

LIGHTEN UP! Count to ten under your breath before jumping in and doing for someone what they're capable of doing for themselves. That practice provides you more time to do what you want to do, and at the same time empowers others to take care of their business. At work, practice sitting back and not being the first to volunteer for a task. There's no shame in being a selfist, remember? For you!

I have control over my life and I allow and support others to do the same!

Today, I intend

1.

2.

3.

I'm so happy and grateful

1.

2.

3.

Day's End

I celebrate

I learned

I would change

*T*omorrow, I look forward to

I AM flourishing! I AM love, health, abundance, joy and success!

> "You aren't perfect and you never will be. Perfect is beige. You're red hot! You don't politely sit on the tables, you dance on them"
>
> –KRIS CARR

My wildest times

_____

_____

_____

_____

Inspired Action

FLOW! Live life with passion and observe how life opportunities open up for you. Has your crazy, impulsive self gone underground? Is your sex life kinda mundane? Experiment; by yourself or with a partner. You are red hot and absolutely comfortable in the skin you're in! When you're happy with yourself it shows and you're in the flow of life.

I'm so absolutely in love with who I am and I have passion for my life!

Today, I intend	I'm so happy and grateful
1.	1.
2.	2.
3.	3.

Day's End

I celebrate

I learned

I would change

*T*omorrow, I look forward to

I AM flourishing! I AM love, health, abundance, joy and success!

"Your surroundings, home, personal care, pets, clothing and body are all reflections of how you see and express yourself. Do these reflect your true self?"

–DR. CHRISTIANE NORTHRUP

*D*o they?

_____

_____

_____

_____

Inspired Action

EXPRESS YOURSELF! Overhaul your surroundings and wardrobe. Get rid of what doesn't express who you are now! Align your appearance, your clothes and your home with who you are and how you see yourself. No need to do it all in one day, take your time and enjoy the process.

How I speak and act is the perfect expression of my true self!

Today, I intend	I'm so happy and grateful
1.	1.
2.	2.
3.	3.

Day's End

I celebrate

I learned

I would change

*T*omorrow, I look forward to

I AM flourishing! I AM love, health, abundance, joy and success!

"Our country needs to learn to measure its strength not by the number of people it can kill but by the number of people it can feed, clothe, house and care for."
–BEN COHEN/JERRY GREENFIELD

The Choice Is Yours

"There are two ways of spreading the light; to be the candle or the mirror that reflects it."

–EDITH WHARTON

EXPLORE, TRANSFORM, FLOURISH COMPANION JOURNAL

"Infinite patience produces immediate results"
–A COURSE IN MIRACLES

*I*nteresting because

_____

_____

_____

_____

_____

Inspired Action

BE PATIENT! It's challenging when we want to see change in our world, now! Remember, this too shall pass, whatever "this' is. Today's quote is a great mantra to help relinquish control and lose the resistance to what is. When you remain calm, confident and faithful, miracles happen, faster than you can imagine. What a paradox!

I know that everything is happening as it should and I accept that some things take longer!

Today, I intend

1.
2.
3.

I'm so happy and grateful

1.
2.
3.

Day's End

I celebrate

I learned

I would change

Tomorrow, I look forward to

I AM flourishing! I AM love, health, abundance, joy and success!

"The planet does not need more 'successful people'. The planet desperately needs more peacemakers, healers, restorers, storytellers and lovers of all kinds"

—DALAI LAMA

I think
_____
_____
_____
_____
_____

Inspired Action

Be love! When you love who you are, what you do, and who you're with, you attract the people and circumstances to fulfill your dreams. Love heals, and when we extend our heart's energy through love, we positively impact our world by raising it's vibration. So, BE love today, and every day! How close are you to living the flourishing life of your dreams?

I vibrate at a high frequency and attract like minded people to my life!

Today, I intend	I'm so happy and grateful
1.	1.
2.	2.
3.	3.

Day's End

I celebrate

I learned

I would change

*T*omorrow, I look forward to

I AM flourishing! I AM love, health, abundance, joy and success!

"Your smile is your logo, your personality is your business card, and the way you make people feel is your trademark"

–JAY DANZIE

*M*y brand is

_____

_____

_____

_____

Inspired Action

BE HAPPY! Would you rather be right or would you rather be happy? Seek out opportunities to join with others today. Acknowledge their opinions and point out what they're doing "right" instead of having to have the last word and correct them or disagree with them. Collaborate rather than compete today!

I AM unstoppable! I have the power to create my life and make a difference in the world.

Today, I intend	*I'm so happy and grateful*
1.	1.
2.	2.
3.	3.

Day's End

I celebrate

I learned

I would change

*T*omorrow, I look forward to

I AM flourishing! I AM love, health, abundance, joy and success!

> "Successful people make money.
> It's not that people who make money become successful,
> but that successful people attract money.
> They bring success to what they do."
>
> –WAYNE DYER

*S*uccess is

_____

_____

_____

_____

Inspired Action

BE GENEROUS! We attract what we are! If you're not fully engaged in your work, consider what position would be the best showcase of your talents AND something you'd love. In the meantime, show up each day as your best self and that creates success. The money and new opportunities will come forth when you love what you do and have an attitude of gratitude for the present. Add to your 'I AM Unlimited ' page and upgrade any limting beliefs.

I AM unlimited in my wealth. All areas of my life are abundant and fulfilling!

Today, I intend	I'm so happy and grateful
1.	1.
2.	2.
3.	3.

Day's End

I celebrate

I learned

I would change

*T*omorrow, I look forward to

I AM flourishing! I AM love, health, abundance, joy and success!

> "Life is all about balance, you don't always need to be getting stuff done. Sometimes it's perfectly ok, and absolutely necessary, to shut down, kick back, and do nothing"
>
> –LORI DESCHENE

I'm healthier and happier

_____

_____

_____

_____

Inspired Action

BE JOY! As we age we tend to lose that childlike sense of wonder and play. Today, see your life through the eyes of a child and bring a childlike innocence and inquiry as well as delight to all you do. Engage in some childhood pastime? Spend time with your children, or offer to spend time with a friend's child. Perhaps volunteering at a school is of interest; double bonus - experiencing more joy and helping children feel special with your attention and time!

I celebrate life and love every day!

Today, I intend	I'm so happy and grateful
1.	1.
2.	2.
3.	3.

Day's End

I celebrate

I learned

I would change

*T*omorrow, I look forward to

I AM flourishing! I AM love, health, abundance, joy and success!

EXPLORE, TRANSFORM, FLOURISH COMPANION JOURNAL

"To forgive is the highest, most beautiful form of love. In return, you will receive untold peace and happiness"

–ROBERT MULLER

My forgiveness challenge is

_____

_____

_____

_____

Inspired Action

BE PEACE! We can't claim we want peace without creating that within our own lives. Adjust your morning and/ or evening rituals to include ways to create peace in your body, your life and relationships. Is there unfinished emotional business to be dealt with? Take steps to resolve those issues. Furthermore don't be 'anti' anything. Be 'for' not 'against' as energy flows where your attention goes.

I allow calm and peaceful energy, thoughts and things to flow easily to me!

Today, I intend	I'm so happy and grateful
1.	1.
2.	2.
3.	3.

Day's End

I celebrate

I learned

I would change

*T*omorrow, I look forward to

I AM flourishing! I AM love, health, abundance, joy and success!

> "Be enthusiastic: I began to realize how important it was to be enthusiastic in life. If you are interested in something, no matter what it is, go at it full speed. Embrace it with both arms, hug it, love it and above all become passionate about it. Lukewarm is not good"
>
> –ROALD DAHL

I'm grateful for what I've learned

_____

_____

_____

_____

Inspired Action

BE ENTHUSIASTIC! Enthusiasm means 'God within'. Step into your power, embrace your life and keep moving forward and upward to greater and greater possibilities. You have all the tools and know how now, in fact you always did. You've transformed your life and shown up as your brilliant self, encouraging others to do the same. Review your pages, and see if there something that needs some attention?

My days begin and end with gratitude. I AM thankful to be alive and on purpose!

Today, I intend	I'm so happy and grateful
1.	1.
2.	2.
3.	3.

Day's End

I celebrate

I learned

I would change

*T*omorrow, I look forward to

I AM flourishing! I AM love, health, abundance, joy and success!

"Gratitude unlocks the fullness of life. It turns what we have into enough, and more. It turns denials into acceptance, chaos to order, confusion to clarity. It can turn a meal into a feast, a house into a home, a stranger into a friend. Gratitude makes sense of our past, brings peace for today and creates a vision for tomorrow"

–MELODY BEATTIE

*M*y life is full

_____

_____

_____

_____

Inspired Action

Be One! We're all connected; this human family of ours. Ask yourself today, and each day: 'How may I serve?' BE quiet and listen; to your heart, to your body, to others. Keep your tank full by making your well being a priority. From this day forward BE a leader and focus on SELF first. A happier, healthier you helps to create a happier, healthier world. Here's to you, thank you! Namaste!

I open my heart to all beings on the planet!

Today, I intend	I'm so happy and grateful
1.	1.
2.	2.
3.	3.

Day's End

I celebrate

I learned

I would change

*T*omorrow, I look forward to

I AM flourishing! I AM love, health, abundance, joy and success!

EXPLORE, TRANSFORM, FLOURISH COMPANION JOURNAL

> "All children have within them the potential to be great kids. It's our job to create a great world where the potential can flourish"
>
> —STANLEY GREENSPAN

If I were a world leader

_____

_____

_____

_____

Inspired Action

BE THE CHANGE! Envision the world you want to live in and then BE that change, leading by example, with your words and actions.

Through your journal exploration you've contributed to the planet by making a difference in your life and those around you. You have the power to change the world by taking care of you first!

Well done! Leaving Normal, Start Where You Are - Begin again!

I AM a living, breathing example of the kind of world I want to live in!

Today, I intend	I'm so happy and grateful
1.	1.
2.	2.
3.	3.

Day's End

I celebrate

I learned

I would change

*T*omorrow, I look forward to

I AM flourishing! I AM love, health, abundance, joy and success!

My Gratitude List

GILLIAN STEVENS

EXPLORE, TRANSFORM, FLOURISH COMPANION JOURNAL

Ya, I'm That Good

GILLIAN STEVENS

EXPLORE, TRANSFORM, FLOURISH COMPANION JOURNAL

What Inspires Me

GILLIAN STEVENS

EXPLORE, TRANSFORM, FLOURISH COMPANION JOURNAL

Notes

GILLIAN STEVENS

EXPLORE, TRANSFORM, FLOURISH COMPANION JOURNAL

GILLIAN STEVENS

EXPLORE, TRANSFORM, FLOURISH COMPANION JOURNAL

GILLIAN STEVENS

EXPLORE, TRANSFORM, FLOURISH COMPANION JOURNAL

GILLIAN STEVENS

EXPLORE, TRANSFORM, FLOURISH COMPANION JOURNAL

GILLIAN STEVENS

www.ingramcontent.com/pod-product-compliance
Lightning Source LLC
Chambersburg PA
CBHW070631220526
45466CB00001B/144